To the teachers and the students; to all who understand that we are always both at once, all in one. –O.R.P.

To Mom and Grandma. I love you, always. –J.J.

Brimming with creative inspiration, how-to projects, and useful information to enrich your everyday life, Quarto Knows is a favorite destination for those pursuing their interests and passions. Visit our site and dig deeper with our books into your area of interest: Quarto Creates, Quarto Cooks, Quarto Homes, Quarto Lives, Quarto Drives, Quarto Explores, Quarto Gifts, or Quarto Kids.

First Published in 2018 by Seagrass Press, an imprint of The Quarto Group.
6 Orchard Road, Suite 100, Lake Forest, CA 92630, USA.
T (949) 380-7510 **F** (949) 380-7575 **www.QuartoKnows.com**

Seagrass Press titles are also available at discount for retail, wholesale, promotional, and bulk purchase. For details, contact the Special Sales Manager by email at specialsales@quarto.com or by mail at The Quarto Group, Attn: Special Sales Manager, 401 Second Avenue North, Suite 310, Minneapolis, MN 55401 USA.

ISBN: 978-1-63322-498-8

Digital edition published in 2018
eISBN: 978-1-63322-499-5

Copy editor: Victoria Robinson

Printed in China
10 9 8 7 6 5 4 3 2 1

Acknowledgments

Infinite gratitude to Kevin Lewis, who is both incredibly large-hearted and phenomenally gifted. It was an honor and privilege to work with him. Each day, I was encouraged, inspired, and educated in myriad ways.

This book owes a great debt to the record left by Clara Luper in her autobiography, *Behold the Walls.* Many thanks also to Ayanna Najuma for sharing her story and memories. Ms. Najuma, at the age of seven, was one of the original sit-inners in Oklahoma City on August 19, 1958. Today, she is the founder of I HAVE A VOICE NOW!, a movement to educate, encourage, and empower young people on the importance of advocacy and activism in order to utilize their own voice for equity and equality in society.

I am forever inspired by and grateful to Clara Luper and the young sit-inners, including Marilyn Hildreth, Calvin Luper, Barbara Posey, Lana Pogue, Linda Pogue, Ayanna Najuma, Portwood Williams Jr., Gwendolyn Fuller Mukes, Richard Brown, Alma Faye Washington, Areda Tolliver, Elmer Edwards, Lynzetta Jones, Goldie Battle, Betty Germany, and all of the young people then and now who sit, march, stand, speak up, show up, and show out for justice.

SOMEDAY IS NOW

Written by Olugbemisola Rhuday-Perkovich

Illustrated by Jade Johnson

SEA GRASS

In the 1930s, when Clara Luper was a little girl, her father promised that someday he would take her to zoos and parks when white people were there and to restaurants where they could sit down and have dinner like any other American.

"Someday will be real soon," her father would say. **"Someday will be real soon."**

Back then, many states denied Black people certain rights because of the color of their skin. Even though Clara's father had served his country during World War I, he returned home to heartache and hate.

Laws in Oklahoma and other states said that Black people and white people had to be segregated. That meant that the law separated Black and white people in many public places.

But there was nothing fair about separating human beings by race. Separate meant unequal.

When her brother got sick, the local hospital refused to care for him. He was turned away because he was Black.

Separate and unequal.

Clara Luper's all-Black classroom had torn books, few supplies, and one person who had to work three jobs: teacher, principal, and janitor!

Separate and unequal.

White people could eat in any restaurant or at any lunch counter. Black people weren't allowed to sit at those tables. They had to stay outside.

Separate and unequal.

Someday seemed very far away.

But Clara Luper's family believed in something bigger than the segregated worlds that small minds made. As Clara Luper grew, she kept learning, reading, and preparing for the someday her father had promised. She wanted to help others prepare for it too, so she became a teacher. Clara Luper told her students that education meant participation. She taught them important lessons about speaking out and standing strong.

"You can't come in and sit there on your constitutional right," she'd say. "You make your changes in this world."

Clara Luper's teaching opened eyes and helped big dreams bloom. A local organization called the NAACP noticed and asked her to lead their Youth Council. They wanted Clara Luper to help Black children learn about their history to build a better future. They wanted her to prepare their children for someday.

Clara Luper wrote a play called *Brother President* about people who spoke out and stood strong for justice, activists like Dr. Martin Luther King Jr. and the protesters in the Montgomery Bus Boycott. The Youth Council children held Clara Luper's words in their hearts and shared her story's power in their performances.

The play was such a success that the NAACP invited Clara Luper and her students to take the show on the road...

...all the way to New York City!

In New York, like in most integrated Northern cities, Clara Luper and her students did not have to eat outside. They could sit at lunch counters and eat with everyone else. They saw Black and white people eating side by side. Everything they ate tasted so good, sprinkled with hope, spiced with justice.

Clara Luper showed her students that in some places, **someday was now.**

After they left New York City, Clara Luper took her students to Arlington National Cemetery in Washington, DC. As they stood in front of the Tomb of the Unknown Soldier, they thought about how soldiers like Clara's father had served their country.

"All of these people died for our freedom," said one girl. "We need to really get busy and do something for our country."

The children wanted to participate in the American story.

Clara Luper took her students back to Oklahoma through the segregated South. They rode the bus through Tennessee and Arkansas and other states where segregation was the law. They passed the WHITES ONLY signs. They ate outside, separate and unequal once again.

But now, the students knew what it was like to sit down at a lunch counter like white children did every day. They had tasted a little freedom.

Clara Luper knew that "a little bit of freedom is a dangerous thing."

"Freedom now! Freedom now!" the students chanted.

When they got back to Oklahoma City, the students remembered Clara Luper's lessons. They remembered Dr. King and the Montgomery Bus Boycott. Then Clara Luper taught them about

**investigation,
negotiation,
education,
and demonstration.**

With these four steps of nonviolence, the students were prepared to make sacrifices for justice.

Clara Luper's students approached local white shopkeepers about opening their stores and restaurants to all people, all the time. The students hoped that their white friends and neighbors would do the right thing if they spoke to them the right way.

WHITES ONLY

Day by day, month after month, for more than a year, Clara Luper helped her students write letters and meet with the shopkeepers.

But those business owners wanted to keep WHITES ONLY.

They did not believe in someday.

The students had done the best they could with the steps Clara Luper had taught them. They had investigated. They had tried to negotiate and educate.

Now, these children were ready to **demonstrate.**

Someday was NOW.

Clara Luper told the parents what their children wanted to do. They would go down to Katz drugstore and drink their Cokes in the seats that Black people weren't allowed to sit in. She reminded the students to bring their books, because no matter what happened, they would keep learning.

Even so, Clara Luper wondered if these children belonged in their homes, safely drinking sodas with their parents, not on the front lines, learning the hard lessons of hate.

At Katz, one of the littlest girls took Clara Luper's hand, and they stepped forward together. The other children followed close behind.

"We'd like thirteen Cokes, please," said another brave young girl.

The waitress told them to take their drinks and go, like it was just another day.

But it wasn't.

Not that day.

That day Clara Luper and her students sat down.

They sat in.

The manager rushed over and told Clara Luper to take her students and get out.

He yelled, "You know better than this!"

He shouted, "You are just a troublemaker!"

"Thirteen Cokes, please," repeated Clara Luper.

Someday was NOW.

White friends and neighbors came to Katz. But they didn't act like friends anymore. Their faces were "cold as Alaskan icicles."

Mothers spat.

Fathers screamed.

People threw food at the children and called them hateful names.

The police arrived and surrounded Clara Luper and the children like they were the dangerous ones.

But Clara Luper and her students just sat and read and studied—and asked to be served.

When Katz finally closed, Clara Luper and her students went home.

But they did not give up. They would be back tomorrow.

That night, hate-filled voices hissed and shouted on Clara Luper's telephone. They threatened violence if she didn't stop.

"Be careful, Clara," said worried family and friends. "Please be careful."

Clara Luper went to bed remembering the ugly words and pushes and shoves of her white neighbors. She wondered if freedom was too dangerous. Would ignorance and hate crush the children's spirits?

But Clara Luper had taught powerful lessons to parents and children alike. She'd taught them to believe, to make the changes they wanted to see.

And the next day, her students came back—with friends. Enough to fill almost every seat!

Someday was NOW.

Clara Luper and her students kept coming back.

They kept sitting and studying and asking to be served.

Even when people shouted

and poured drinks on their heads

and threw food

and spit ugliness and hate.

The children kept on sitting and studying and asking to be served.

After years of segregation, months of student preparation, and days of student demonstration, Katz announced that all of its lunch counters—

in Missouri,

in Kansas,

in Iowa,

and in Oklahoma—

would serve all people

of every race.

Clara Luper had taught her students that they could "stand, and stand strong"—

even when sitting.

And when that special day came, that day when they could sit down in Katz and have their first burgers and Cokes right there—

inside—

it tasted so good!

It tasted like hope

and power

and liberty and justice for all.

They ate and drank

and talked and laughed

and read and studied and dreamed.

And then...

More About Clara Luper

Clara Luper wasn't born with that last name; Luper came later, after she got married. But the Clara Luper who inspired children was always inside of her. Clara Luper was born Clara Mae Shepard in Okfuskee County, Oklahoma, in 1923. Her mother was a laundress and her father was a laborer who had served with the American Expeditionary Forces on the Western Front of World War I. After attending segregated schools where "we'd be reading sometime on page four, and the next page would be ten," Clara went on to become the first African American admitted to the University of Oklahoma's graduate history program. She received her master's degree in 1951. A scholarship is now offered at Oklahoma City University in her name.

In addition to being an author, activist, magazine publisher, and educator, she was the first Black woman to be named an honorary Oklahoma County sheriff, and she hosted a radio talk show for twenty years.

> "Somewhere I read, in the Fourteenth Amendment, that I was a citizen and I had rights, and I had the right to eat." – **Clara Luper**

In 1958, Clara Luper led a group of around a dozen young people, aged 6 to 17, to conduct a lunch counter sit-in at Katz drugstore in Oklahoma City.

After Katz agreed to desegregate its 38 stores, Clara Luper and the NAACP youth spent the next six years desegregating other local businesses. In 1964, the Oklahoma City Council outlawed discrimination in public accommodations because of race, religion, or color. "Within that hamburger was the whole essence of democracy," Clara Luper remembered.

A year and a half after Clara Luper and the Oklahoma City children successfully integrated the Katz lunch counters, college students in Greensboro, North Carolina, launched a series of lunch counter sit-ins that sparked a national movement.

In 1969, Clara Luper was named a spokesperson for Oklahoma City sanitation workers who went on strike to protest low pay, poor treatment, and difficult working conditions. Clara Luper and some sanitation workers were jailed for blocking a garbage truck. The city agreed to most of their demands and the strike ended after almost four months.

> "You make your changes in this world." – **Clara Luper**

When she ran for the U.S. Senate in 1972, she was asked if she, a Black woman, could represent white people. Her answer: "Of course, I can represent white people, black people, red people, yellow people, brown people, and polka-dot people. You see, I have lived long enough to know that people are people."

> "Even a young child can lead." – **Clara Luper**

Sometimes called "Mother Luper," Clara Luper's influence as a lifelong teacher and leader inspired people of all ages to take direct, nonviolent action for civil rights. One of her former students, Joyce Henderson, said, "She made each of us feel special, like she was our mother."

She taught in Oklahoma public schools for more than 40 years and served on the Oklahoma City school board, where she promoted the teaching of Black history in schools. In 2018, the Department of African American Studies at the University of Oklahoma was named in her honor.

For Clara Luper, education was empowerment. I called them my diamonds," said Clara Luper about her students in an interview. "You gotta dig for a diamond. You gotta polish it." While friends and classmates were given toys for Christmas, Clara Luper's children got books. She woke her daughter Marilyn in the mornings with the question, "Do you want to continue your education today?" Marilyn recalls her mother's commitment to training and discipline. "She was able to train young people to do almost anything... She would tell us: Anything that you can dream, you can achieve."

Clara Luper died on June 8, 2011. She had a vision for breaking down what she called the "invisible walls" that continue to divide us, and she lived it. Clara Luper told her story in the book *Behold the Walls,* published in 1979. She shared her passion for justice with a group of young people in Oklahoma City, and that legacy is offered to all of us today. Don't just "sit there on your constitutional right!" What are your dreams for a just world? How will you achieve them?

> "Anything you can dream, you can achieve." – **Clara Luper**

Steps of Nonviolent Resistance

© The Oklahoman

In *Behold the Walls,* Clara Luper reviews the steps that she learned and then taught her students. These were the steps that they used to successfully desegregate Katz and other lunch counters:

- **Investigation:** First, get the facts of the situation. Don't move forward on guesses and assumptions. Make sure that an injustice has been done.

- **Negotiation:** Go to your opponents and make your case. Maybe your opponents are unaware of the problem, so let them know that you're willing to work with them on a solution, but you are going to continue to work for justice.

- **Education:** Be sure that you and your team know all of the facts of the issues you're working on. Remind them that change doesn't come easy, but change for justice must come.

- **Demonstration:** After all of the previous steps have been taken, if they are not met with success, this is the final step. Nonviolent demonstration needs to be organized and disciplined. Participants must remain calm and be ready to sacrifice with dignity. Everyone should know that suffering is "part of the nonviolent approach. It is to be endured, never inflicted." In the end, this approach will give activists "the moral victory upon which the eternal struggle for Freedom, Justice, and Equality can be won."

© The Oklahoman

Glossary

Activist: a person of any age who is working for social change. Activists can write letters, sign petitions, demonstrate, make speeches, march, and do many different things to campaign to bring about changes in different areas of society.

Arlington National Cemetery: a military cemetery founded in 1866, and located in Arlington County, Virginia, that honors veterans who served in major United States conflicts.

Constitutional Right: a freedom that is officially and legally guaranteed to be protected. "Freedom of speech" is a well-known part of U.S. citizens' First Amendment Constitutional right to assemble, establish a religion, petition the government, and distribute information or opinions through the press without restrictions from the government.

Dr. Martin Luther King Jr.: an American Baptist minister and activist who became one of the most prominent leaders in the civil rights movement from 1954 through 1968. He was one of the founders of the Southern Christian Leadership Project (SCLC) and was called on to be the spokesperson for the Montgomery Bus Boycott. Throughout his life and work, King promoted the use of nonviolent direct action as an effective way to eliminate injustice. He was the winner of the Nobel Peace Prize in 1964, saying that "I believe that unarmed truth and unconditional love will have the final word in reality." On April 4,

1967, one year before he was assassinated, he spoke at Riverside Church in New York City, saying that, "The greatest purveyor of violence in the world today—my own government." On another occasion, he pointed out that the country needed more than just "change": "I think you've got to have a reconstruction of the entire society, a revolution of values." He began a "Poor People's Campaign" to support those in poverty, and he expressed his opposition to the Vietnam War.

He was killed on April 4, 1968, in Memphis, Tennessee, where he was appearing in support of sanitation workers who were protesting unjust working conditions. In 1983, his birthday was named a federal holiday, and it was first celebrated as such in 1986.

Injustice: unfairness; a violation of someone's rights.

Integrated: combined or united; putting people together and offering equal opportunity and conditions to all.

Montgomery Bus Boycott: a campaign of resistance against Montgomery, Alabama's segregated public transit system. The widespread boycott was sparked by the actions of NAACP activist Rosa Parks and led by the Montgomery Improvement Association with Dr. Martin Luther King Jr. as spokesperson. The boycott lasted 381 days. African Americans who participated were threatened with violence, jailed, and many lost their jobs. They persisted, and in 1956, the U.S. Supreme Court declared

segregation on public buses to be illegal. It was a seminal event in the civil rights movement.

NAACP: the National Association for the Advancement of Colored People (NAACP) is a civil rights organization founded in 1909 to promote equality and justice for all citizens and to fight racially motivated discrimination and violence.

NAACP Youth Council: a branch of the NAACP that engages young people in social justice. It was started in 1935 by Juanita E. Jackson, who later became known as the first Black woman to practice law in the state of Maryland.

Segregation: setting apart from other people or things. From 1896 to 1954, the United States government enforced a legal system of separating African Americans from whites commonly called Jim Crow. Activists challenged these discriminatory laws for many decades. In 1954, the Supreme Court ruled that "separate but equal" public schools were against the law. The Civil Rights Act of 1964 made segregation in public places illegal. *De jure segregation*, which is segregation by law, is illegal in the United States. *De facto segregation*, the fact of the practice of segregation, remains.

Tomb of the Unknown Soldier: or the Tomb of the Unknowns, is a monument dedicated to U.S. service members who have died but have never been identified. Inscribed on the back of the Tomb are the words "Here rests in honored glory an American soldier known but to God."